ISBN 978-1-5284-1303-9
PIBN 10908885

Forgotten Books is a registered trademark of FB &c Ltd.
Copyright © 2018 FB &c Ltd.
FB &c Ltd, Dalton House, 60 Windsor Avenue, London, SW19 2RR.
Company number 08720141. Registered in England and Wales.

For support please visit www.forgottenbooks.com

The institute has attempted to obtain the best
original copy available for filming. Features of this
copy which may be bibliographically unique,
which may alter any of the images in the
reproduction, or which may significantly change
the usual method of filming, are checked below.

L'Institut a microfilmé le meille
qu'il lui a été possible de se pro
de cet exemplaire qui sunt peut
point de vue bibliographique, q
une image reproduite, ou qui p
modification dans la méthode i
sont indiqués ci-dessous.

☑ Coloured covers/
Couverture de couleur

☐ Covers damaged/
Couverture endommagée

☐ Covers restored and/or laminated/
Couverture restaurée et/ou pelliculée

☐ Cover title missing/
Le titre de couverture manque

☐ Coloured maps/
Cartes géographiques en couleur

☐ Coloured ink (i.e. other than blue or black)/
Encre de couleur (i.e. autre que bleue ou noire)

☐ Coloured plates and/or illustrations/
Planches et/ou illustrations en couleur

☐ Bound with other material/
Relié avec d'autres documents

☐ Tight binding may cause shadows or distortion
along interior margin/
La reliure serrée peut causer de l'ombre ou de la
distorsion le long de la marge intérieure

☐ Blank leaves added during restoration may
appear within the text. Whenever possible, these
have been omitted from filming/
Il se peut que certaines pages blanches ajoutées
lors d'une restauration apparaissent dans le texte,
mais, lorsque cela était possible, ces pages n'ont
pas été filmées.

☐ Additional comments:/
Commentaires supplémentaires:

☐ Coloured pages/
Pages de couleur

☐ Pages damaged/
Pages endommagées

☐ Pages restored and/or lam
Pages restaurées et/ou pei

☑ Pages discoloured, stained
Pages décolorées, tacheté

☐ Pages detached/
Pages détachées

☑ Showthrough/
Transparence

☐ Quality of print varies/
Qualité inégale de l'impres

☐ Includes supplementary m
Comprend du matériel sup

☐ Only edition available/
Seule édition disponible

☐ Pages wholly or partially o
slips, tissues, etc., have be
ensure the best possible im
Les pages totalement ou pa
obscurcies par un feuillet d
etc., ont été filmées à nou
obtenir la meilleure image

This item is filmed at the reduction ratio checked below/
Ce document est filmé au taux de réduction indiqué ci-dessous.

10X	14X	18X	22X	26X

28X

LIST

OF

VOTERS

FOR THE

TOWN OF GODERICH,

1876.

LIST OF VOTERS
FOR THE TOWN OF GODERICH, 1876.

No. 1 Sub-Division.

Conseq. No.	No. on Assm't Roll.	NAME.	Freeholder Householder or Tenant.	No. of Lot
		A		
1	1	Armstrong Henry	H	232
2	2	Allan Walter D.	F	Con C pt 11
3	3	Allan Alex. McD.	H	1175,1158, 1159, 11.., 1176, 1174, 1161, 1172
4	4	Allan D.	F	1175, 1158, 1159,1160, 1173, 1174, 1161,1172
5	5	Andrews James	F	322
6	9	Archibald Chas. E.	H	323
		B		
7	11	Butler John	T	122
8	12	Biddulph George	F	1384,1383
9	13	Bencom John	F	1399
10	15	Brindley John	H	1146
11	17	Bullman Wm.	H	1108
12	26	Barry Fred	H	827
13	96	Brockenridge Jas. McN.	F	1133,1120
14	157	Brigham John E.	T	124
		C		
15	28	Campbell Robert	H	128
16	29	Cassady Thomas	F	1209,1210
17	30	Charlton Mathew	F	269
18	31	Cattle George	F	270
19	32	Clucas Henry	T	174
20	33	Cameron M. C.	F	174
21	34	Cassady Isaac	F	1371,1372
22	35	Cathcart Alexander	H	1102
23	36	Campbell John	F	1102
24	37	Campbell Donald	F	McDougall Survey 2
25	39	Cox William	T	171
26	40	Crabb Christopher	F	320,321
27	166	Campbell David	F	1111
		D		
28	43	Dart Andrew	H	1220,1221
29	44	Donivan Donald	F	1220,1221

30	45	Donogh John	F	1200,1201, 1202, 1203
31	46	Downing Ephraim	H	828
32	16	Doyle B. L,	F	1146

E

33	48	Ellis Joseph	F	G W S 5,25
34	49	Elliott William	F	424
85	50	Edwards Edwin	H	128
36	53	Edwards John H,	F	1068
87	56	Edwards Jas. B	H	1187
38	58	Elliott James	F	G W S 31,8,9,10,11,28, 29,30
39	59	Edwards Joseph	F	Con C. B. 12
40	00	Emerton John	F	McDougall Surv. 1,89

F

41	62	Ferguson Francis	F	1188

G

42	63	Goodall Andrew	F	866,867
43	64	Gibbons Robert	F	Con A pt 8
44	66	Graham George	F	481
45	67	Gibson Samuel	H	1131,1132
46	47	Graham Edward	F	828

H

47	72	Headly Wm.	F	1152
48	75	Herr Joseph	F	420,421
49	76	Henderson Alex	F	1094,1095
50	77	Hunter Wm	H	1107
51	79	Halcrow John	F	McD S 15,16
52	80	Hincks Harvey	F	McD S 11,29,10,80
53	81	Holland Thomas	F	do 4,36
54	82	Horton Horace	F	1164, 1165, 1170, 1171, 1169, 1163, 1162, 1166, 1167,1168

J

55	84	Johnston Joseph	H	pt 208
56	86	Jardine William	H	Gordon Survey 5
57	88	Johnston Thomas	F	McD S 19,20,21
38	145	Johnston John	F	869

K

59	92	Kay William	F	825
60	93	Keag James	F	1151
61	94	Keag William	F	1134
62	126	Knight William	F	1072

L

63	97	Lindsay Nixon	H	Maitland Con 107
64	209	Lamprey Wm.	F	G W S 7,27

M

65	99	Murray David	F	1114,1115,1116
66	100	Murray William	F	2,22, G W S
67	101	Moorehouse T. J.	F	422, pt 423
68	102	Millar W. R.	F	1147,1149
69	104	May Richard	H	278
70	106	Mitchell James	F	1104
71	107	McQueen Allan	F	1075
72	109	McMahon George	F	Con C 14
73	111	McMullen John A.	F	1216,1217,1218,1219

74	112	McKendry Daniel	F	1198,1199
75	113	McKenzie Robt Wm.	H	1100,1101
76	114	McLean Robert Jur	F	1100,1101
77	115	McKenzie Mark	H	pt 225
78	117	McCeag Samuel	H	pt 428
79	119	McGrattan Hugh	H	Con A pt 8
80	120	McTear John	H	1145
81	121	McCue Thomas	F	1391,1392,1393,1394
82	122	McClellan John W.	F	1096,1097,1098
83	123	McVicar James	F	1069
84	124	McVicar Adam	F	1071
85	125	McVicar John	H	1072

N

86	129	Nicholson Angus	F	1178,1179,1180
87	130	Nicholson Wm.	H	873
88	132	Newell John	F	1385,1386

O

89	133	Orr Robert	F	1190,1191

P

90	138	Piper William	H	pt 1106 pt 1165

R

91	142	Robertson George	F	1226
92	143	Rusk James	F	1248
93	144	Reid Samuel	H	369
94	146	Reed Harry	H	pt 222
95	148	Roberts Robert	H	pt 222
96	150	Ross Rev. J.	H	pt 828
97	152	Ross William	F	1387,1388
98	153	Ross Hugh	F	1080 pt 1079
99	184	Reid Wm.	F	Con C 11 pt

S

100	154	Seymour Wm.	F	McD S 17,18,22,23,24 25,26,47,49,50,51,52
101	155	Seymour Bartholomew	F	McD S 53,54,55,56,57, 58,59,60,88,84,62,61,74
102	156	Seegmiller Fred	T	124
103	159	Sharman Robert	F	1223
104	160	Stotts Wm.	F	219
105	161	Stotts Edward	F	220 pt 268
106	162	Smith Abraham	F	318,319,326
107	163	Skimmings Jas.	F	pt 221
108	164	Skimmings Wm.	F	173
109	165	Suelden Robert	H	1111
110	167	Sturdy Oswald	H	1222
111	169	Startin Thomas	F	1198
112	170	Street James A.	H	pt 225
113	172	Shepherd James	T	pt 128
114	173	Strachan Donald C.	T	pt 128
115	174	Schroeder Wm.	F	1367,1368,1369,1370
116	175	Salkeld Isaac	F	Con C pt Block 12
117	176	Sproul John	F	1117
118	178	Stuthers Gavin	F	G W S 3,23
119	180	Sloan Samuel	F	Mait Con pt 107 & 108
120	181	Saunders James	F	1187,1189

T

121	182	Thompson Robert	F	824 pt 872
122	171	Thomson James	F	pt 225
128	183	Thomas Charles	H	Con O pt 11
124	187	Swaffield Wm.	F	1109

W

125	189	Wallace Alex.	F	172
126	190	Whitley Wm. Y.	H	173
127	194	Winters Samuel	F	1183
128	195	Whitley Robert J.	F	Gordon S 1,2,3,4
129	196	Wily Arthur	H	271
130	198	Weatherald Thos.	F	426,427,428,429,430
181	201	West Frederick	H	pt 123 pt 122
182	202	Wilson Wm.	F	1141,1142
183	208	Wells Henry	F	Con O Lot 9
184	205	Wells Charles jnr.	F	1889,1890
185	206	Wilson Wm.	F	1118,1119
186	208	Waters Martin	H	G W S 7,27
187	210	Wilson Lockman	F	Mait Con 107
188	10	Whitley Joseph	F	828
189	68	Wilson Robert	F	1181,1182
140	181	Whitley John	F	878

Y

| 141 | 215 | Young Richard | F | 827 |

No. 2 Sub-Division.

Consec. No.	No. on Assessm't Roll.	NAME.	Freeholder Householder or Tenant.	No. of Lot

A

142	218	Addison James	F	1341,1331,1842
143	219	Adam William	H	18, 15 cedar street
144	221	Allan Robt. Gallespie	F	1886
145	226	Aitkin John	H	pt 181
146	428	Andrews James	F	pt 279

B

147	229	Brooks Wm.	F	pt 1810
148	230	Barret Thomas	F	6 Maitland Road
149	231	Brown James	F	24,25 cedar street
150	232	Bates George	F	1846,1847
151	233	Brooks James	F	882
152	284	Bell Henry	F	1887
153	287	Black Robert C.	F	pt 137
154	288	Buchanan Allan	H	140
155	240	Bates Charles	F	241,242
156	241	Baumstalk John	F	12 Con A
157	242	Bunbury H. T.	F	83,84
158	243	Breckenridge John	F	13, 14 Con A
159	816	Black David A.	F	40,41,81
160	488	Brown Henry	T	pt 70

C

| 161 | 245 | Cressman Moses | H | pt 276 |
| 162 | 247 | Campbell Daniel | F | 75 |

162	248	Clucas Henry	F	pt 130
164	249	Cook James	F	1816
165	250	Chalwell John	H	1,29 cypress street
166	252	Connors John	H	1350
167	253	Crabb C.	F	70
168	254	Crawford Hugh	H	1827
169	253	Garey Lucius	F	1343,1344,1359,1360
170	257	Carman Robt	F	283
171	258	Cowherd Thomas	F	240
172	259	Craig James	F	286,337
173	260	Calback W. A.	H	77
174	262	Clark Henry	H	2 Mait con
175	267	Campbell Neil	T	pt 70
176	304	Clifford Edwin	F	pt 87
177	314	Cattle George	F	40,41,81

D

178	271	Dyett Bobt	F	12,13,14 cedar street
179	273	Downing Ephraim	T	pt 27
180	274	Downing John	T	pt 27
181	276	Dancey Thomas N.		7
182	278	Duckham John		88
183	280	Dickson James		
184	281	Dickson Wm		B
185	317	Detlor J. V.		31
186	318	Detlor S. H.		31

E

187	284	Elliott Lewis	F	73
188	285	Edwards Thos R.	F	85
189	286	Elliot Giffard	T	pt 70
190	288	Evans George	F	pt 12 Con A

F

191	291	Fulford Robert	F	136
192	292	Fields James	H	pt 182

G

193	284	Grace Wm. E.	F	pt 140
194	285	Gooling W. F.	F	1861,1862
195	286	Graham Ed,	F	pt 80
196	287	Graham George	F	1307
197	288	Greenwood W. E.	H	49
198	255	Graham James	F	1827

H

199	290	Hodge Archibald	F	pt 12 Con A
200	294	Hyslop John	F	pt Block D.
201	295	Hall Thomas	H	pt 71
202	297	Herr Joseph	F	pt 276
203	298	Horton Henry	F	43
204	300	Humber Chas A.	F	1317,1326
205	301	Hale Hezekiah	H	331
206	303	Higgins Michael	H	pt 87
207	305	Hosker Ed.	F	555,632
208	311	Horton Horace	F	40,41,81
209	320	Hilliard W. M.	T	pt 27
210	320	Hayhoe Rev. Mr.	T	pt 70
211	326	Hazleton Eliaa	F	1834,1809
212	327	Hurley Patrick	H	90

213	288	Harrison Herbert	F	pt 12 Con A
214	842	Hincks Harvey	F	179
215	852	Horton Henry sr,	F	pt 176

J

216	830	Johnston Thomas	H	pt 125
217	835	Johnston Thomas jur.	H	72

K

218	888	Kerr Robert	F	1856 pt 1857
219	889	Kendrick ———	H	pt 12 Con A.
220	841	Knox John	H	179
221	289	Kyle Richard	F	49

L

222	846	Lutit James	F	88
223	847	Lawrason W. C.	H	1338

M

224	849	Mitchell John	F	pt 11 Con A
225	850	Miller James	F	88
226	858	Mann Frederick R.	F	pt 29
227	854	Murney W. H.	F	13,14
228	855	Morrow Robert	H	1,28 Cypress street
229	857	Mains William	H	8 Maitland Road
230	861	Million James	H	281
231	863	Mathews Wm. B.	H	85
232	865	Million George	H	pt 86
233	220	Martin James	F	15,16 cedar st
234	877	McGregor Wm.	H	pt 126
235	879	McLean Allan P.	F	pt 31
236	880	McLeod John	F	482
237	892	McPhail Malcolm	F	190
238	882	McLeod John	F	pt 11 Con A
239	885	McKeag William	F	178
240	886	McManus Chas.	F	pt 182
241	889	McLean Robert sur.	F	129
242	891	McLean Thos. F.	F	pt 12 Con A
243	892	McIntosh John & Co.	T	pt 70
244	227	McLean Robert jur.	F	pt 131
245	828	McCarthy Pat	F	80
246	866	McCutcheon Robert	F	pt 86
247	462	McIntosh Wm.	F	89
248	465	McKay James	F	89

N

249	867	Nolan Peter	F	126
250	868	Neelon Michael	F	21,8 Cypress street
251	870	Neibergall Balser	H	234
252	872	Nesbitt Robert	H	82

P

253	895	Parsons G. H.	F	28
254	896	Peck Leonard	H	pt 176
255	898	Proudfoot Robert	H	pt 80 pt 1018
256	408	Publow George	H	1329
257	802	Porter John	F	881
258	871	Potts William	F	234

R

249	407	Robertson Edward	F	79
260	408	Robertson W. R.	H	pt 87

261	412	Riley Michael	H	pt 282
262	414	Russell John	F	84
263	415	Reed Wm	H	pt 125
264	268	Ransford Henry	F	pt 2 Maitland con.
265	807	Runciman Robert	F	40,41,81
266	809	Runciman David	F	40,41,81

S

267	420	Stewart George	H	pt 181
268	424	Smith Abraham	F	pt 125
269	425	Smail James	F	88,76
270	426	Strachan Donald	F	pt 180
271	427	Simmonds Robert	H	pt 279
272	429	Saunders James	T	pt 70
273	431	Scott James	H	pt 129
274	433	Spence Henry	F	180
275	436	Scikeld Wilson	F	pt 81
276	440	Stewart John	F	182
277	441	Seegmiller Fred	F	1364, 1828, 1830, 1365, 1854.1840,1852,1868 &c.
278	446	Speight Fredk.	F	1823,1824
279	447	Siemous James	F	pt 185
280	448	Shannon Ed.	F	pt 185
281	449	Shepherd Albert	F	137
282	450	Standly R. W	F	pt 12 Con A
283	451	Story James	H	pt 12 Con A
284	453	Sturdy John L.	H	181
285	491	Swanston Magnus	F	pt 138
286	279	Swanston George	F	pt 188
287	810	Smeeth Francis	F	40,41,81

T

288	457	Troy Thomas	F	227
289	458	Toms Isaac F.	F	pt Block D
290	459	Twitchell Ed.	F	274
291	460	Tichbourne Richard	F	pt 226
292	461	Trull Henry	H	89
293	464	Todd Alex.	H	89
294	466	Thomson James	F	Block C
295	831	Trueman G. M.	F	125

W

296	469	Wilson Abraham	H	42
297	471	Williams Joseph	F	82
298	475	Whitley James	F	275
299	476	Watson Isaac	H	pt 226
300	478	Wilson Robert	F	15,16,17, Pine st. 12,18, 14 Cypress street
301	479	Wyatt Thomas	F	12,13 Huron Road
302	480	Woodman Joseph	H	26 Cypress street
303	481	Wilson Benjamin	F	26 do
304	482	Winter Robert	F	5 Maitland Road
305	483	Wilson Jonathan	F	8 Pine Street
306	484	Ward Stewart	H	831
307	485	Weatherald John W.	F	831
308	486	Williamson Andrew	H	184 A
309	487	Whitley John	F	184 A
310	468	Wright Wm.	H	184 A

371	490	Warmer Sam	x	pt 138
312	494	Walters Wm.	x	pt 128
313	495	Whitley Mark	r	pt 128
314	204	White W. M.	r	1829

Y

| 315 | 496 | Young Richard | r | pt 11 Con A. |

No. 3 Sub-Division.

Consec N'o	No, on Assessm't Roll.	NAME.	Freeholder Householder or Tenant.	No 19 '69. of Lot

A

316	497	Andrews Stephen	x	pt 933
317	498	Acheson George	F	pt 933
318	499	Anderson O. G.	H	888
319	501	Armstrong Richard	H	pt 548
320	503	Acheson William	r	pt 878
321	504	Adams David.	F	884
322	505	Arthur Wm	H	pt 858
323	507	Arthur Wallace	T	pt 858
324	518	Armstrong J. D.	r	860
325	596	Allan Anthony	r	pt 857
326	509	Armstrong David	T	859
327	510	Armstrong Ed.	T	859
328	511	Armstrong Ben	T	859

B

329	514	Bond John	T	pt 966
330	516	Bates John	r	942
331	517	Bissett James	x	pt 1008
332	518	Brooks James	F	pt 989
333	519	Brough Secker	H	947
334	521	Breckenridge John	F	pt 952
335	522	Brown Joseph	F	549
336	523	Barry George	T	905
337	619	Baily James	T	857 pt

C

338	525	Campbell Wm.	F	1012
339	526	Crofts Benjamin	H	908
340	528	Caldwell James	T	pt 906
341	530	Colborne J. H.		Income
342	531	Cooke Henry	T	pt 933
343	533	Curry John C.	T	pt 933
344	535	Cameron M. C	T	pt 966
345	602	Campbell Robert	r	949

D

346	537	Davis Geo. N.	F	904
347	538	Detlor Jno. V.	F	914,945
348	539	Dougherty Wm.	H	pt 1001
349	540	Doyle Sylvester	H	1078
350	548	Duncan Jno T.	H	pt 376
351	544	Detlor S. H.	H	pt 979
352	555	Dixon Thos.	x	861

353	706	Dancey, Thos. N.	F	976
		E		
354	546	Evans George	F	1016
		F		
355	549	Ferguson Daniel	T	pt 905
356	553	Fletcher Chas.	H	pt 876
357	554	Feetham Wm.	H	861
358	556	Frazer Donald	H	943
		G		
359	558	Garrow James T.	T	pt 934
360	559	Garside Samuel	H	973
		H		
361	465	Horton Horace	F	877
362	566	Horton Henry	T	pt 966
363	569	Holmes Daniel	F	pt 1007
364	570	Hunter John	H	pt 1011
365	572	Hood Wm.	H	pt 983
366	574	Hick Walter	F	919
367	576	Hadden Archd.	F	pt 855
368	690	Howell Harvey	F	934
369	718	Hutton William	F	955
		J		
370	580	Johnston E. L.	F	863, 864, 886, 887
371	581	Jenkins James	H	941
		K		
372	584	Kerr Dawson	T	934
373	586	Kirkbride Alex	H	946
374	588	Knox John	T	pt 879
		L		
375	591	Lindsay, Nixon	T	pt 934
		M		
376	593	Michie Peter	H	pt 869
377	595	Mills Richard	T	857
378	597	Morris Fred'k	H	857
379	599	Mitchell James	H	964
380	600	Mitchell John	F	964
381	601	Morris Kenneth	H	949
382	603	Mitchel John (Tailor)	H	pt 907
383	605	Moore E. F.	F	921
384	606	Mitchell Wm.	T	pt 935
385	611	Miller Chas. E.	F	pt 883
386	612	Martin Elijah	F	969
387	613	Martin Jno. O.	H	937
388	616	Mair Thomas	H	625
389	618	Martin Allan	H	pt 857
		Mc		
390	626	MacKay Robert	F	854
391	627	McKenzie Robert Wm.	T	pt 934
392	628	McLean Allan P.	F	934
393	630	McMath Hugh	H	pt 869
394	633	McMath Samuel	F	part 1008 pt 1007
395	635	McQuarry Alex	F	part 944
396	636	McQuarry Malcolm	F	pt 944
397	637	McKeown Wm.	H	973
398	639	McLennan Martin	H	970

399	640	McKenzie John	F	906 pt
400	641	McLean Robert jur.,	F	pt 906
401	642	McKenzie George	H	pt 907
402	644	McIntosh Chas.	F	950
403	645	McKenzie Thos.	F	pt 883
404	649	McConnell John	F	pt 1001
405	571	McKenzie Mark	F	pt 1011
406	592	McLean Wm.	F	pt 934
407	608	McConnell David	F	pt 935

N

408	721	Noble Samuel	H	938
409	622	Neighbergall George	H	547
410	624	Noble Philo	T	pt 878

O

411	650	Olds Geo. W.	T	pt 934
412	651	O'Dea Patrick	F	pt 934

P

413	652	Payne John	H	908
414	657	Payne James	H	pt 548
415	659	Pentland Thomas	F	912
416	500	Potts Wm.	F	888

R

417	660	Rothwell Wm.	T	856
418	661	Robertson W. R	T	pt 934
419	663	Rhynas Robt.	F	pt 980
420	664	Runciman Robt	F	629, pt 630
421	666	Rothwell Thos Henry	H	pt 1010
422	668	Rumball Wm	H	pt 974
423	672	Ralph John	T	pt 966
424	675	Robinson Wm.	H	pt 879
425		Robertson George	F	pt 1001
426		Robertson Ed.	F	pt 1001
427	506	Ross James	F	pt 881 pt 858
428	677	Sloan Samuel	F	880
429	679	Salts William	H	917
430	681	Sneyd Thomas	H	pt 908
431	683	Sharman Ed.	F	pt 975
432	684	Sharman William	F	pt 975
433	685	Secord Horatio	H	pt 979
434	686	Shannon William	H	1008
435	688	Smith Abraham	F	pt 966
436	691	Savage W. M.	F	pt 983
437	693	Smith William	F	1020
438	695	Savage John	H	974
439	697	Sinclair Colin	H	pt 880
440	699	Sharman William	T	pt 935
441	701	Straubel Charles F.	T	pt 935
442	703	Sutton George	H	pt 878
443	716	Smeeth Francis	F	865
444	545	Story John	F	pt 979
445	607	Swanston Magnus	T	pt 935
446	731	Sinclair James S.	T	pt 905
447	705	Thomson Geo. W.	H	976
448	707	Trueman Geo. M.	F	880 pt
449	709	Tomlinson James	F	pt 553, 550, 551, 552, 554

450	711	Tronch Frank	F	pt 970
451	712	Thompson John	H	985
452	714	Taylor Alexander	F	916
453	715	Torrington John	F	907
454	717	Whitely Robt. J.	F	968
455	718	Waddington Wm.	F	pt 553
456	719	Wynn John	H	pt 630
457	720	Westrope Thos.	H	pt 1003
458	722	White Wm. M.	F	pt 973
459	724	Warmer Ben	H	881
460	726	Wetherald John W.	T	pt 926
461	730	Wade Ed. E.	T	pt 905
462	733	Wade Mark E.	H	1003
463	735	Wright James	F	pt 868
464	736	Walker Robt.	T	pt 868
465	536	Whitely James	F	966
466	552	Wallis John	F	1009
467	614	Whitely Thomas	H	987
468		Wilson Ben	F	pt 1001
469	737	Van Every Thos. B.	F	909,940

No. 4 Sub-Division.

Consec. No.	No. on Assess'nt Roll	NAME.	Freeholder Householder or Tenant.	No. of Lot
		A		
470	739	Acheson John	F	765 Pt 766
471	740	Andrews Wm.	F	817,840
472	741	Adam Alexander	H	Pt 811
473	743	Acheson Wm.	F	742,743
		B		
474	744	Bates Robert	F	745,690
475	745	Bates Thomas	F	Pt 689
476	746	Brown Wm. G.	H	Pt 841
477	748	Black David A.	H	Pt 786
478	750	Black Robert	F	Pt 77,9
479	751	Buchanan James	F	717,718,737
480	754	Boosey Wm. J.	F	596
481	755	Bell Alexander	F	592
482	773	Bissett Wm.	F	Pt 733
483	881	Butler John	F	613,614,536,537
		C		
484		Campagne Nesbit	F	587
4	369	Craig Wm.	F	786
4 3	756	Connors James	F	789
4 7	757	Campbell Neil	H	790
4 3	759	Cash Wm.	H	790
4	761	Coleman Patrick	F	Pt 786
490	762	Crny Michael	F	Pt 696
491	763	Campaigne Ed.	F	1063
492	764	Cameron M. C.	F	639, 640, 648, 649, 647, 650, 637, 688

493	791	Cantelon Arthur	F	Pt 767
494	811	Calbeck Arthur	F	725
495	765	Detlor Thos. D. W.	F	758

D

496	766	Downing John	H	784
497	767	Dodd Henry	F	727
498	768	Dunn John	F	595
499	769	Davis Patrick	F	515
500	830	Dancey Thos. N.	F	513,614,536,587

E

501	771	Ervin Isaac	F	816,889
502	772	Eagle Alex	F	726

F

503	774	Fairbairn Jas. R.	H	Pt 841
		Fisher David	F	768
504	829	Fisher Samuel	F	788

G

505	777	Girvin John	H	pt 788
506	779	Goodall John	H	591,590
507	781	Griffin Gerry	F	583

H

508	783	Howell Harvey	F	667,686,703,704
509	784	Hyslop James	H	722
510	785	Henley John	F	594
511	786	Hyslop Robt	F	509
512		Henderson Robt	F	682
513	871	Henning Wm.	F	pt 764, pt 762

J

514	787	Johnston Jas. J.	F	804
515	788	Jamieson John	H	pt 783
516	790	Johnston Wm. E.	H	pt 767

K

517	792	Kerr Dawson	H	pt 766

L

518	794	Lawson David	F	702
519	795	Lamont John	F	582
520	803	Land E. K.	F	835

M

521	796	Millen James	F	513
522	798	Morton Alex.	H	818
523	799	Martin Wm.	F	769
524	800	Mills Richard	H	785
525	802	Martin James	H	838
526	804	Martin Isaac	H	841
527	806	Martin John	F	787
528	749	Martin Henry	F	788
529	810	McQuarry John	H	725
530	812	McKenzie Alex.	F	750
531	813	McIntosh Chas.	F	713,782,783
532	814	McIntosh Chas. A.	F	pt 713,712,714
533	815	McKee George	H	pt 835
534	817	McPherson Finlay	H	pt 621
535	819	McMullen Chas.	F	819
536	821	McLean Thos. F.	F	782
537	822	McFarlane John	H	pt 788

538	824	McKay John	H	pt 766
539	826	McLeod Duncan	H	705
540	829	McCroath	H	724
541	831	McGregor A. M.	F	715
542	882	McAvoy John	F	pt 678 pt 660
543	835	McIntosh Jno. C.	F	pt 696

N

| 544 | 866 | Noble Philo | H | 720 |
| 545 | 838 | Nairn John | F | 744 |

O

| 546 | 840 | Old G. W. | F | pt 767 |
| 547 | 841 | O'Rourke Peter | F | 701 |

P

548	842	Prindeville Ed.	H	pt 699
549	844	Pollock Samuel	F	pt 762
550	845	Passmore John	F	739, 740
551	846	Pridham John	F	741
552	847	Platt Samuel	F	700
553	848	Payne Charles	F	593

R

554	849	Radcliff Richard	H	719
555	850	Robinson James	F	760
556	852	Rothwell Wm.	H	723
557	854	Roberts John	F	pt 706
558	855	Robinson W. J.	F	761
559	856	Reid James	F	673
560	857	Robinson W. J. *Sailor*	H	pt 786

S

561	859	Seager Charles	F	589
562	860	Savage W. M.	F	841 pt
563	861	Strachan David	F	pt 811
564	863	Somerville Wm. J.	H	pt 783
565	867	Strang Hugh W.	H	829, 805
566	868	Stewart Wm.	H	786
567	870	Somerville Jno. B.	F	764, 763
568	873	Stoddart David	F	746
569	874	Shannon G. C.	F	646
570	875	Scott Wm. B.	F	684
571	877	Swift Dean	F	1066
572	878	Strachan Donald	F	618, 614, 586, 587
573	879	Shepherd James	F	618, 614, 586, 587
574	808	Sloane Samuel	F	pt 699
575	827	Seymour Wm.	F	pt 705
576	828	Seymour Bart.	F	705
577	887	Spence Henry	F	720

T

578	883	Thrower Wm.	F	693
579	884	Tremble	F	588
580		Taylor Alexander		Income

W

581	885	Worden Wm.	F	707, 691, 692
582	886	Williams Joseph	F	619, 620
583	890	Walker John	F	pt 621
584	891	Weller Samuel	F	677
585	892	Watson James	F	662, 675

586	801	Wells Henry	F	785
587	816	Wells Charles	F	835
		Y		
588	893	Yates Stephen	H	499,500
589	895	Yates James	F	669
590	897	Young Alex.	F	683

No. 5 Sub-Division.

Consec. No.	No. on Assessm't Roll.	NAME.	Freeholder Householder or Tenant.	No. of Lot
		A		
591	898	Acheson John	T	pt 1000
592	899	Acheson George	F	pt 1000
593	900	Armstrong Henry	T	pt 1000
594	902	Armstrong Robert	H	pt 796
595	904	Adamson Peter	F	873
596	905	Armstrong Edward	H	pt 900
597	907	Adams Rodney	H	1 office reserve
598	909	Addison James	H	X A 12,11,10,7,5,6, 8,9, office reserve
599	910	Annis Andrew	F	493
600	911	Austin George F.	H	480
601	912	Allan W. D.	F	S
		B		
602	913	Bruce John	F	925 pt 924
603	914	Buchanan Daniel	H	pt 956
604	916	Buchanan James	F	pt 848
605	982	Black James	F	1 t 900
		C		
606	919	Clark Robert	F	560
607	922	Currie John C.	H	pt 990
608	923	Crofts Benjamin	F	pt 924
609	924	Craig William	H	1048
610	925	Cockburn John	H	478
611	926	Campbell	T	pt 965
612	927	Campbell James	F	pt 965
613	928	Campaigne Godwin	F	pt 1000
614	930	Curren Samuel	H	pt 960
615	932	Costie William	H	pt 953
616	934	Craigie John	H	pt 561
617	939	Cassaday John	H	pt 899
618	941	Craig John, sr,	F	20 & 21 office reserve
619	920	Clark John	F	560
620	1012	Crabb G.	F	1033,1027
		D		
621	942	Davis G. N.	F	964
622	943	Dickson Archy	F	pt 999
623	944	Dunlop Hugh	F	pt 997
624	947	Detlor J. V.	F	1028, 1029
625	948	Detlor S. H.	F	1032
626	949	Detlor John C.	T	pt 930

627	950	Detlor Thomas D. W.	T	pt 950
628	952	Doyle James	F	872
629	953	Doty Darius	F	897
630	954	Doyle B. L.	T	pt 929

E

| 631 | 956 | Elwood Rev. E. L. | H | 802,803,828 |

F

632	957	Finlay Jas. H.	H	pts 999,999,962
633	958	Fuller Norman	H	986
634	961	Fields John	H	1054,1060

G

635	962	Graham Johnston	F	992
636	963	Grant George	2	pt 965
637	964	Gordon Daniel	F	pt 999,938
638	965	Globensky Alfred	H	pt 995
639	966	Gale Alfred	H	pt 927
640	967	Grace W. E.	F	1040,1041
641	968	Garrow James T.	H	847

H

642	971	Horton Herace	F	485,486,569,570
643	972	Hutty Frederick	H	pt 965
644	973	Horton Joseph	H	pt 926
645	974	Horton Henry, sr.	F	pt 926
646	975	Hassard William	H	pt 957
647	979	Hamilton Hugh	H	pt 994
648	981	Hammell Thomas	H	pt 900
649	983	Hayes James	H	pt 2 office reserve
650	984	Herr Joseph	F	pt 2
651	985	Hutchinson M.	H	898
652	987	Hutton William	F	797
653	988	Hawley Richard, sr.	F	1045
654	1050	Hay David	F	953

J

655	989	Johnston F. W.	T	pt 999
656	992	Jones Edward	F	991
657	993	Johnston George B	F	871
658	994	Johnston Hugh	F	570, 573, 572, 571, 487 488,489,490,491
959	995	Jordan Francis	F	pt 929
660	996	Jordan Alfred	F	pt 894
661	1017	Johnston Thomas	F	960
662	987	Johnston B. B.	T	pt 929

K

663	998	Knight William	T	pt 1000
664	1001	Kneeshaw Albert	R	pt 958
665	1002	Kirkpatrick R. H.	F	989
666	1008	Kidd Thomas	H	751
667	1011	Kneeshaw Alexander	F	pt 893

L

| 668 | 1007 | Lefler Solomon | H | 4 office reserve |
| 669 | 1010 | Lee William | H | 893 |

M

670	1013	Moore Edward S.	T	pt 930
671	1016	Moore David	H	pt 960
672	1018	Mitchell Wm.	H	pt 926

673	1020	Moore Henry J.	H	pt 896
674	1022	Mathewson John	H	pt 927
675	1023	Murray Allan	F	pt 479
676	1024	Moorehouse T. J.	T	pt 980
677	1026	Munro Alexander	F	pt 926
678	1029	Morton Alexander	H	pt 848
679	1031	McEwen Peter	T	1026
680	1033	McEwen George	T	1035 pt 1036
681	1035	McLean William	F	577,578
682	1039	McArthur John	F	pt 899
683	1040	MacKay Robert	F	pt 999
684	1041	MacKay Daniel C.	F	567
685	1042	McCormick Bernard	H	pt 926
686	1044	McBrien Robert	F	pt 870
687	1045	McBrien Johnston	F	pt 870
688	1047	McNamara William	F	954
689	1048	McLeod Murdock	H	pt 502
690	1049	McLeod Donald	H	953
691	1051	McLeod Donald	F	477
692	1053	McIver Angus	H	994
693	1055	MacDermott Henry	F	W
694	1056	McFadden W. H.	H	pt 929
695	1058	McCara John	F	576
696	1059	McIntosh J. C.	F	pt 927
697	1060	McDougall John S.	H	850
698	1061	McIntosh John, jr.	F	pt 899

N

699	1062	Nicholson Malcolm	F	pt 996
700	978	Naftal John Thos.	F	922

O

701	1063	Ogilvie & Hutchinson	F	1039,1042,1043

P

702	1064	Parson George H.	F	1064
703	1066	Pharis John W.	T	998
704	1068	Phillips William	F	997
705	1069	Pretty Charles	H	pt 927
706	1071	Parson James G.	F	987
707	1072	Polley A. M.	F	901

R

708	1074	Reeves Phillip	T	pt 995
709	1075	Robertson Charles E.	F	568
710	1077	Ross A. M.	F	752,753,754,775,776

S

711	1078	Smith Harry H.	T	pt 1000
712	1081	Simmons Richard	F	995
713	1082	Squier W. R.	F	492,575
714	1085	Smith W. G.	F	pt 996
715	1086	Seegmiller Frederick	F	pt 958
716	1087	Stewart James	H	pt 870
717	1090	Stewart John	F	564
718	1092	Seymour William	F	1087,1086
719	1092	Seymour Bart.	F	1087,1086
720	1097	Smaill James	T	pt 929
721	1100	Sinclair James S.	F	827,799,800,801, 825,826

722	1101	Stanely R. W.	r	1084
723	1103	Sneyd Thomas	r	895
724	986	Savage W. M.	r	pt 898

T

725	1102	Trainer B.	H	895
726	1104	Thompson Robert R.	x	pt 995
727	1105	Tolsma Sebe	N	pt 1044

V

| 728 | 1106 | Vivian James | r | 1000 pt |

W

| 729 | 1108 | Welsh William T. | T | pt 1000 |
| 730 | 1117 | Watson E. R. | r | pt 931 |

No. 6 Sub-Division.

Consec. No	No. on Assessm't Roll.	NAMES	Freeholder Householder or Tenant.	No. of Lot

A

| 731 | 1121 | Allan Alex. McD. | T | pt 69 |
| 732 | 1124 | Allan W. D. | F | 303,304 |

B

733	1125	Ball John	T	pt 69
734	1127	Ball Stephen	T	90 142
735	1130	Ball Henry Wm.	H	pt 68
736	1134	Boice Richard H.	F	209
737	1135	Bain Hugh	F	158
738	1136	Black William	F	301
739	1137	Bain John	H	258
740	1139	Bonsorry Richard	F	pt 359
741	1140	Brown John R.	H	266
742	1144	Bingham Edwin	H	pt 69
743	1145	Blake John	F	pt 69
744	1147	Burke James	F	365
745	1151	Breckenridge John	F	pt 25
746	1153	Burke Samuel	F	200

C

747	1146	Cooke Henry	H	365
748	1148	Campbell Wm.	F	159
749	1149	Curren Samuel	F	pt 65
750	1150	Cantelon David	H	pt 25
751	1152	Carroll Michael	F	17
752	1153	Clissold Joseph	F	18
753	1156	Cantelon Arthur	F	205
754	1157	Campbell Robt.	H	200
755	1159	Campbell Lachlan	H	352
756	1160	Campbell Daniel	F	352
757	1161	Cox William	H	121
758	1286	Cassady John	F	94,95
759	1318	Clack Colin	F	105

D

| 760 | 1164 | Davis G. N. | F | 199 |
| 761 | 1165 | Dickson Avery | F | 10,11 |

762	1166	Davison John	F	307,109
763	1167	Dobbie John C.	F	169
764	1168	Doty Darius	T	pt 26
765	1170	Donald James	H	164 A
766	1172	Dancer Thos N.	F	
767	1174	Davis Jefferson	F	22
768	1175	Doyle B. L.	H	100
769	1176	Dickson James	F	344, 345, 346, 295, 299, 297
770	1122	Dickson James S.	T	pt 69
771	1177	Fiddler Humphrey	F	pt 199
772	1178	Ford Peter	F	394, 395
773	1285	Ford George	F	64
774	1254	Gordon Daniel	F	96
775	1179	Gibbons Wm.	H	97
776	1185	Granger Robt.	H	pt 115
777	1187	Grace W. B.	F	66, 67, A. 67 B
778	1188	Galloway James	H	191
779	1190	Goodall Andrew	T	pt 69
780	1192	Howland Chas.	H	147, 98
781	1193	Haldane John	F	149, 98
782	1195	Henley Edward	H	68
783	1196	Hay David jur.	F	117
784	1197	Heally Thomas	F	161
785	1199	Heale James	F	247
786	1200	Hood Thomas	F	pt 310
787	1202	Hawley Richard	F	St. Christoper Beach
788	1203	Hicks Edw J.	H	pt 26
789	1205	Johnston F. W.	F	109
790	1206	Johnson G. B.	T	pt 26
791	1208	Johnston Alex.	F	259
792	1209	Jones Edward	H	415
793	1188	Jones Wm.	F	258
794	1210	Kirkpatrick Jno. C.	F	340, 291
795	1211	Kay William	T	pt 26
796	1273	Kirkpatrick R. H.		
797	1212	Lawrence Frank	H	pt 22
798	1214	Longworth John	F	800
799	1215	Lewis Ira	F	58, 59
800	1221	Lawson Alex.	H	197
801	1218	Marlton Henry	F	91
802	1219	Moore Elijah	F	204
803	1220	Murray Malcolm	H	197
804	1222	Mahony Timothy	F	800
805	1223	Marsh Fredk	H	255
806	1224	Miller John R.	F	pt 310
807	1225	Mathews Alex.	H	pt 216
808	1226	McKay James A.	F	307, 308, 309

809	1227	McBrion Johnston	F	169
810	1228	McKay Wm S.	F	207
811	1229	McPhail Daniel	F	248,249
812	1282	McKay Eric	F	28
813	1287	McKenzie Donald	F	pt 118
814	1288	McGillivray Rev. A.	H	118
815	1270	McPherson John	H	212
816	1242	McMicking Geo. M.	F	210,261
817	1243	McLeod John	H	206
818	1244	McKenzie Alex.	F	201
819	1246	McKenzie Roderick	F	149
820	1247	McPherson Murdock	F	141,145
821	1248	McCarthy Thos.	F	298,299
822	1250	McCallum	F	pt 859
823	1252	McKenzie R. W.	F	6

N

824	1253	Neilson Samuel	H	96
825	1255	Nunn Philip	E	55
826	1180	Nicholson Malcolm	F	97

P

827	1259	Percy Stephen	H	267
828	1261	Parsons Geo. H.	F	245,246,194,196
829	1262	Polley A. M.	F	pt 167
830	1265	Patterson Donald	F	252
831	1266	Payne James	E	257

R

832	1270	Radcliff Richard	F	part 12
833	1271	Rutson Thomas	F	16, 61
834	1272	Ryckman David	H	4
835	1274	Reid Jamieson	F	412
836	1276	Robinson W. J.	F	406, 407
837	1277	Reid David	F	862, 814
838	1278	Read John	F	413
839	1279	Robertson F. A.	F	15
840	1280	Robertson W. H.	F	69
841	1281	Rattenburry Isaac	F	57
842	1282	Ross A. M.	F	161, 13

S

843	1183	Simmons Richard	F	235
844	1284	Seymour Wm	F	94, 95
845	1285	Seymour Bert.	F	150
846	1289	Simmons Rich'd sr.	F	165
847	1290	Shanklin Gilbert	H	116
848	1292	Simmons Alex. J.	T	pt 26
849	1294	Swanston George	F	208
850	1296	Somers John	H	410, 411
851	1297	Somers Wm	F	417
852	1298	Savage W. M.	T	pt 60
853	1800	Story John	T	pt 26
854	1302	Stotts Ed.	F	170
855	1803	Smith Abraham	F	817
856	1804	Shepherd James	F	414
857	1213	Slack Chas. E.	F	166

		T		
858	1189	Turner Henry E.	F	191
859	1805	Toms Isaac F.	H	244, 193, 192, 213
860	1807	Tait James	F	202
861	1808	Tisdale James	F	405
862	1809	Thompson R. R.	T	pt 69
863	1181	Trueman G. M.	T	pt 68
864	1171	Taylor Robert	F	164 A
		V		
865	1821	Videan Thomas	F	19
		W		
866	1812	Watson Dixie	T	pt 26
867	1814	Wallace Alex	F	pt 25
868	1815	Wiggins James	F	9
869	1816	Wiggins Eri	F	104
870	1817	Ward W. H.	H	105
871	1822	Willoughby John	H	56
872	1824	Waddell Andrew	H	111
873	1826	Walker F. F.	F	100
874	1827	Watson Wm.	F	203
875	1828	Wells Lambert	H	267
876	1880	Watson Alex	F	217, 218
877	1881	Williams Jas. H.	T	pt 120
878	1884	Watson James	F	pt 120
879	1885	Whitely John	H	119
880	1887	Wilkinson James	F	815
881	1806	Wilson Byron	F	148
		Y		
882	1888	Young Robert	F	114
883	1256	Young Wm	F	55

No. 7 Sub-Division.

		A		
884	1839	Andrews Stephen	F	4 Con A.
885	1840	Andrews Thomas	F	W S 74,39,40,41,42,43
886	1475	Allan Walter D.	F	6 Con C.
		B		
887	1842	Bolton Henry	F	R. S. 74
888	1843	Bluett Fredk	H	W S 78
889	1844	Baxter James	F	W S 86,85,104
890	1845	Bartliff James	H	pt 5 Con A
891	1846	Ball John	F	pt 5 Con A
892	1848	Brophy John	F	W S 84,85
893	1851	Blake Joan	F	1227
894	1852	Blake Charles	F	1265,1266
895	1853	Bingham Edwin	F	1,2 Con C
		C		
896	1854	Coutts Gordon	H	W S 110
897	1856	Craig James	F	W S 117,119, 148
898	1857	Cottle Richard	T	pt 5 Con A
899	1859	Craigie Alex.	H	R S 83
900	1861	Cragie James	F	R S 41
901	1862	Cornell Augustus	F	1288,1284
902	1863	Cox George	F	1808, 1804, 1805, 1806, 1268

D

903	1864	Dickson Walter	H	1278,1279
904	1866	Dixon Thomas	F	R S 18,19
905	1867	Dark Henry	H	1271,1272,1301,1302
906	1871	Durnian John	F	W S 128
907	1872	Dausford Chas. E.	F	W S 152,115, 116, 149, 150,151
908	1887	Dunlop Hugh	F	R S 20
909	1441	Detlor S. H.	F	R S 27,28,39

E

| 910 | 1878 | Ellard Luke | F | pt 5 Con A |
| 911 | 1865 | Elliott Lewis | F | 1278,1279 |

F

| 912 | 1884 | Ferguson Daniel | F | 1276,1277 |

G

913	1877	Gordon James	F	W S 12,18,14,28,24,25
914	1878	Grace W. E,	F	16 Con C
915	1880	Garbe Henry	H	W S 123,124,125,142
916	1881	Grierson Wm.	F	V S 61,62,51,52
917	1882	Green James	F	W S 54,59
918	1888	Greenache Joash	H	1276,1277

H

919	1886	Hunter George	H	R S 20
920	1888	Hays James	F	W S 29,80,65,66,46
921	1889	Huckstep Thomas	F	W S 7,8
922	1890	Hopper Edward	F	W S 44,45
923	1891	Halliday Archibald	F	1294,1295
924	1892	Hedger John	F	1290,1291,1293
925	1893	Halliday Isaac	F	1244,1245,1246
926	1895	Johnston G. B.	F	R S 1,2,8,4,6,7,8,9,10
927	1893	Johnston Harry E.	F	R S 11,12,18,14,15,16,17
928	1400	Jordan Francis	F	1 Con A
929	1470	Johnston Hugh	F	19,20 Con C

K

| 930 | 1401 | Kerr William | H | 6,7 Con A |

L

| 931 | 1403 | Lee John | F | W S 27,28 |

M

932	1404	Moss Wm.	F	W S 72,73
933	1406	Marlton Ed.	F	W S 102,103
934	1408	Morrison John	F	R S 7,8
935	1413	Mitchell John	F	1285,1286
636	1417	Mitchell John	F	W S 4,5,6 32
937	1422	McIvor Angus	F	W S 95,96
938	1423	McIvor Murdoc	F	W S 97,98,99
939	1425	McFarline James	F	4. 5. con. A
940	1427	McMurphy Archy	F	W S 7,112,118,114
941	1429	McDonald Alexander	F	pt 5 con A
942	1434	McDiarmid Alex.	F	W S 127,188,189
943	1435	McKay Neil	F	W S 147
944	1440	McEwen Peter	H	R S 27,28,29
945	1442	McKinnon Neil	F	W S 9,10,11
946	1448	McLean Malcolm	H	W S 49,50,63,64
947	1449	McLean Wm.	F	W S 49,50,63,64
948	1450	McKinnon Donald	F	W S 67,68,69

949	1451	McLeod Norman	H	W S 71
950	1452	McEwen Joseph	F	1296,1297
951	1454	McGmatton Hugh	T	5 con C
952	1456	McDonald, Hon. Donald	F	pt 5 con A
953	1358	McDonald Angus	F	5 con A
954	1402	McFarline Peter	F	6, 7 con A
955	1459	Parsons G. H	F	1273,1274
956	1450	Papst Samuel	F	1280,1281,1282
957	1355	Pharis John	F	W S 110

R

958	1461	Robertson Edward, sr.	H	R S 6, 48
959	1462	Robertson W. H.	F	R S 6, 48
960	1468	Reid John	F	W S 120,121,122,143 144,145,146
961	1415	Rattenbury Isaac	F	15 con C

S

962	1466	Stiven William	F	R S 17,18,35,36
963	1465	Sharman William	F	1261, 1262
964	1465	Somers Wm.	H	19,20, con C
965	1471	Stowe Henry	F	1240,1241
966	1472	Smith Abraham	F	W S 15,16,17,18,19, 20, 21, 22.55,56
967	1368	Slack Charles E.	F	1271, 1272, 1301, 1302

T

968	1473	Tierney Patrick	F	pt 5 con A
969	1474	Toepper John G.	H	6 con C

V

970	1477	Videan John	F	W S 105, 106, 107, 108
971	1482	Viles John	F	1287, 1289, 1288

W

972	1476	Watson Dixie	F	pt 5 con A
973	1478	Watson Wm.	F	1238,1299,1254,1255
974	1484	Wilson Johnston	F	1286,1287

I, James Thomson, Clerk of the Municipality of the Town of Goderich, in the County of Huron, do certify that the foregoing list is a correct list of all persons appearing by the Assessment Roll of the said Municipality of the Town of Goderich for the year 1876, entitled to vote at elections for members of the House of Commons and the Legislative Assembly of the Province of Ontario. And I further certify that a copy of the foregoing list was first posted up in my office on the seventh day of August, 1876 ; and I hereby call upon all electors to examine the said list, and if any omissions or other errors are perceived therein, to take immediate proceedings to have the said errors corrected according to Law.

JAMES THOMSON,

Town Clerk.

Dated August 7th, 1876.

CPSIA information can be obtained
at www.ICGtesting.com
Printed in the USA
BVHW031147021118
531990BV00020B/1383/P

9 781528 413039